Bloom Like Nature

Live the Natural Way

Cheryl Lunar Wind & Friends

Bloom Like Nature

Live the Natural Way

Copyright © 2024 by Cheryl Lunar Wind

Cheryl's poetry in this collection may be shared, printed with credit given to the author. All other contributors keep rights to their work. Any Inquiries contact:

cheryl.hiller@yahoo.com

Some of the poems in this collection first appeared in Follow the White Rabbit, We Are One, We Are Forever, Star Messages, Return to Innocence, and Love Unconditional chapbooks; Mount Shasta Bio-Regional Ecology Center newsletter, the Lemurian Revival, Spring 2024 and on facebook.

Front cover photo unknown source, online.

First edition.

Published by Alexander Agency Books, Mount Shasta, California 96067

ISBN 979-8-9897287-4-9

Bloom Like Nature

Live the Natural Way

Dedicated to all humanity.

Preface

Bloom Like Nature carries some of the deepest messages that I have ever delivered. This collection describes the nature of our reality: past, present and future.

Several poems delve into the in-between, a field of consciousness that is intelligent.

They also deal with the belief that all things in nature are alive and sentient.

Animism is defined as the belief that all material phenomena have agency...that the soul, spirit or sentience exists not only in humans but in other animals, plants, rocks, mountains, streams and all nature.

In many cultures and spiritual belief systems people call upon the animals, trees, land and waters to protect and assist them. Examples of this are when indigenous peoples call on the spirit of the Eagle to send and receive messages to the gods, and prayers to the spirit of water for rain, and to the spirit of the land for plentiful harvests.

"Nature never fails."* Therefore, we can go to her for support and refreshment from whatever our version of nature is; it could be gardening, camping, beekeeping, fishing, bird watching, skiing, sitting, walking, swimming or just getting your feet wet at the local watering hole.
*Cody Ray Richardson

"I cannot leave it; I must stay under the old tree in the midst of the long grass, the luxury of the leaves, and the song in the very air. I seem as if I could feel all the glowing life the sunshine gives and the south wind calls to being. The endless grass, the endless leaves, the immense strength of the oak expanding, the unalloyed joy of finch and black bird; from all of them I receive a little. Each gives me something of the pure joy they gather for themselves. In the blackbird's melody, one note is mine; in the dance of the leaf shadows the formed maze is for me, though the motion is theirs; the flowers with a thousand faces have collected the kisses of the morning. Feeling with them, I receive some, at least, of their fullness of life."
---**Richard Jefferies, The Life of the Fields (1884)**

Contents

Everyday by Wolf Martinez 1

The Voice We Remember 2, 3
by A'Marie B. Thomas-Brown

Same but Different 4
by Cody Ray Richardson

We Are One by Cheryl 5

Bloom Like Nature by Cheryl 6

Your Turn to Walk 7
by Cody Ray Richardson

Dying of Love by Maria Louisa 8

Density of Love by Maria Louisa 9

Goddess of Wolves by Mary Schrack 10

A Love Poem by David Kolden 11

What's Happening by Cheryl 12, 13

It's Befuddling by Barbara Bader 14

Feel Good by Julie Bailey 15

In Between by Cody Ray Richardson 16

Present by Mercy Talley 16

In-Between by Cheryl 17

The Field by Maria Louisa 18

We Are the Key by Cheryl 19

The Day the Rainbows Surfed Malibu 20, 21
by Tara Gardner

Trees 22, 23
by Cyrena Giordano/CYRENITY

A Wildfire has it's Purpose 24, 25
by Cody Ray Richardson

Let Me Introduce You to my Red-headed Friend 26
by Karuna McAllister

A Strong Single Woman 27
by Christine Jamison

OUTER-INNER by Maria Louisa 28

Hour Glass 29
by Cody Ray Richardson

What is, is what will be 30
by Cody Ray Richardson

It is what it is by Cheryl 31

Please Keep It by Cheryl 32

Gone by Cheryl 33

Looking at Flowers 34, 35
by Zachary Brown

A Cycle of Love 36
by Cody Ray Richardson

A Poem to Mount Shasta 37
by Tara Gardner

Bring It! by Cheryl 38

Earth Day Gratitude 39
by Patricia Carreras

Hawkwomyn by Mercy Talley 40

Owl by Dave Harvey 40

Not Without Choosing 41
by
Connie Bonner-Britt   Blackfeet name,
Turtle Woman   gifted by sister
Spo- pi- Aakii   Cheryl Ibarra
                          Piegan Woman
                          Pikuni Aakii

Replenishing 42
by Jennifer Hershelman

Experience 43
by Cody Ray Richardson

Contributors page

Author page & Testimonials

Everyday
by Wolf Martinez

Good Morning, Beautiful Day and Evening to you.

No matter what is happening for you, may you
make time to reflect on the things you are grateful
for, let it sink deep into your bones.

Solutions tend to be revealed when I do that.

We remember who we truly are when we go into
the heart, center
and use this blessed mind in good ways.

Talk to the Four Directions, Ancestors, Mother Earth
and Great Spirit about the way you aspire to be in this
world.

Pray for those you are having trouble with (especially ourselves)
for peace, freedom and unity with the precious humanity which
we are all One.

With more Joy, Love and Laughter have Fun and be more Light!

The trees, wind, water, fire; our Mother Earth and all Beings
that live upon her under Father Sun...
are all singing for us because they Love Us.
Listen...you will hear.
Everyday. Everyday.

Mitakuye' Oyasin

The Voice We Remember
by A'Marie B. Thomas-Brown

The smoke has lifted
The New Day has dawned

A robe and Its master
A new quest it's on

Marry the Morrow
In yesterday's pain
A match made in Heaven
A cyclical rain

Now is the time
We are the ones
His and Her comfort
The Daughters and Sons

Light enters Darkness
Ignorance dissipates
The Lion and Lamb
Symbolically ate

666
The mark of the feast
When the Higher and Lower
Come to agree

When eyes are opened
And ears feel the beat
The flutter of justice
From Its ethereal seat

When Truth comes a-marching
Wisdom stands at Her gate
Her children come flocking
To the call of the Eight

The Voice we remember
Within all the noise
Of chaos and comfort
The gift of the ploy

Standing in Light
Radiant Sun and Moon
Clusters of midnight
Whispers of Noon

Hear in the distance
What beats in the heart
One body, one mind
Spirit impart

The remembrance
That what was
Will always be
All is One

Same but Different
by Cody Ray Richardson

It's not back there
It's not up ahead
Though you may look
It isn't to be found
Memories and imagination
Videos in the mind
What will be
What once was
Same in ways
Different in others
One thing in common
Both not real
Only one reality exists
It is now
Lay in it
Swim in it
Push it away
Fall in it
Fly in it
Hold it tightly
A gift
A curse
A blessing
A sentence
Now is what you have
Embrace it
Love it
Hate it
It isn't yours to possess
It is yours to feel
Yours to experience
You made this
It made you
Accept it
Don't accept it
It will change you
You will change it
It is you
You are it
One and the same
Same but different

We Are One
by Cheryl

We are the Many
and We are One.

Flock--
of birds.
Symphony--
of notes.
School--
of fish.
A parade.
Rose garden.
Ant colony.
Mandala. Mosaic. Puzzle.

Deck of cards.

The Multi-Verse---
parallel universes
Stacked
like a deck of cards.

Many of the same thing
same but different.

Like slant rhyme in poetry.
sounds like
but not.

Humanity---
Our similarities and differences
are the same---
Same dramas---
different families.

We are the Many
and We are One.

Bloom Like Nature
by Cheryl

oubaitori- the Japanese idea that people, like flowers, bloom in their own time and in their individual ways.

---Nature is uncensored beauty and raw grit.

---Our mother and father.

---The perfect mix of feminine and masculine.

She is soft, caring, providing and sustaining.

He is strong, intense, detailed and powerful.

Humanity is
on the cusp--
   the edge--
   the precipice.

Nature is our salvation---
Only by returning to the natural way
will we survive.

Know that--
AI is an impostor
attempting to replace the real.
Do not be fooled.

Nature never fails.
She does not need replaced.
Follow her lead, and
you will be
All Right.

Bloom Like Nature.

Your Turn to Walk
by Cody Ray Richardson

Every peace of earth is a grave yard
Every blade of grass an antenna
Sacred is everything
Let your bare feet touch your ancestors
Your turn to walk is honored
Remember who you are
Remember who you were
The soul has no color
Because it is all colors
What comes from the earth will go to the earth
What comes from the stars will go to the stars
The illusion of separation
The order is organized for you
Smiles can be felt
The flowers bloom to touch the feeling
Your tears water their roots
We are one
Though different
The ability to tell is intelligence
The ability to accept is a key
No need to turn it
It has always known there is no lock
It's only the mind that created such a thing

Dying of Love
by Maria Louisa

Like a rose
With petals falling
I stand
In Your Presence.

Exposed to the Holiness
Penetrated wholly
By Life
I am unable to stop
This gentle dismantling.

Such a beautiful way
To die.

**Approaching Threshold
Conscious Being with Dying
As all turns towards God.
--Maria Louisa**

Density of Love
by Maria Louisa

The Density of Love
Vaster than the sky
A holy presence to be attended to
A silence that's
Louder than a cry

Not you or I
or you and me
But We

A love that is expansive
And exists to be free

A grace that winds
And flows
And speaks

Returns to source
Undulates and peaks

Sings happy songs
And together with us cries
Holding hands and
Embracing sighs

Eternal One
That is All in all
Guide us now
And forever more.

Goddess of Wolves
by Mary Schrack

Today,
I am a Native American woman,

with heart and soul---

To Know who I am.

Just a woman, to live today
with peace and harmony.

Today,
I am just a woman,
But that doesn't mean
that I don't love me.

I am New today,
the very best
I can be.

A Love Poem
by David Kolden

What if I told you...

That you have a radiant sweet
presence in your smile.

That you look adorable with
your ponytail, smooth bangs
and pretty sparkly eyes.

That your soul, while manifesting
a child-like vulnerable wide-eye innocence,
contains enough wisdom to fill ten lifetimes.

That your presence is a wondrous source of
comfort and inspiration.

That when I look at you, I think of cute fuzzy
baby ducks.

That you give my life a whole new meaning.

What's Happening
by Cheryl

Every once in a while
you just have to fall apart----
When you pick yourself up, and
put the pieces back together,
you become a different picture.

Falling apart
is something
that
happens often
for me---
lately.
Like every
other day.

The in between
days---
are
for re-assembly,
construction.

In Jenga,
the goal
is the collapse---

We collapse---
to regroup, remake,
revisit---
the who we are
becoming.

The fall---humanity has fallen---
And it was a choice.

How we go back together---
is also a choice.

Ashes, Ashes
We all fall down.
We are

the phoenix rising
out of the ashes.

Do not fear the falling,
do not fight it---
It is necessary.

Necessary evil?
We may not understand it---
want it or choose it---
But it is not evil,
just another stage
in the cycle
of evolution.

For growth
there must be
change,
shattered, broken open---
parts and pieces.

Then the building
can happen---
will happen---
The happening.

It's Befuddling
by Barbara Bader

What if I told you...

flowers are songs, nature is grace and
a droplet from mighty Mt. Shasta flows
far to the ocean?

That a broom can be an inspirational dance partner---

That sunshine streams from grace---

That my muddy path is inspirational---
dank and dark transformed into
bitchin and awesome.

That Spring's beautiful effervescent
harmony can also be dark and dank---

Yet, sunshine's flowing vibrations
give transforming energy.

It's befuddling.

Feel Good
by Julie Bailey

awesome, peaceful, satisfying

what if I told you
that the energy in here is so
"feel good" to me that
I just don't feel like writing.

In Between
by Cody Ray Richardson

The highs are high
The lows are low
In between
Only you know
A place to rest
To take a breath
Past meets future
They make amends
Moving forward
To greener pastures
Away from hurt
Slow heals faster
A smile from a stranger
Tasks done
Some battles lost
Other wars won

Present
by Mercy Talley

I've been
Here
for so long now
but I'd rather
be There
in the Realm
of Heart Knowing

what is the
Present anyway...
but the ebb & flow
of Breath
like an ocean
wave calling
me Home ~

In-Between by Cheryl

What happens
'Between the Telling and the Listening'?

Where does the healing magic happen?
Do we go somewhere else?
Elsewhere.
What else is there?

What do we become?
The becoming---
Listen and learn.
Remember.
Do you ever wonder?
Wander--about, around
life.
Hop, jump and skip
around,
Go on a walk about.

Round and Round we go.

The Field
by Maria Louisa

Conscious (water) vibrations
What does conscious vibration
look like?
a field that knows
Listening to the field
Love which flows...

So much is emerging now concerning
the Field,
the space in between...
Collaboration, flow... we
are moving into a new era of
working together...
One Mind One Love

We Are the Key
by Cheryl

The Event
is not based on the external--
<u>what</u> or <u>when</u>
will the Sun bring it.

When we reach
the level of awareness,
a certain frequency
that will trigger
the Event.

We carry the codes,
that just need switched on--
Enough of those 'lights' being
turned on--
tell Mother Earth, Father Sun and
all the Universal family
that we are ready.

We Are the Key.

The Day the Rainbows Surfed Malibu
by Tara Gardner

Waves crash into the
rocks below
and explode into a
column of water that
leaps above my head.

Seafoam,
bright white
and thick as meringue
dances, reaching higher,
joyful, free of the ocean.
My spirit dances with it.

At its peak
a flash of a rainbow.
As my eyes try to hold
its image and identify the
colors (why does yellow and red
come after blue and green?)
the water falls back
into the ocean.

The shore is transformed
into an iridescent sea of milk,
shimmering, churning.

One wayward wave
surprises me, drenches me.
At first frightened like a child,
quick tears,
and then giggles.

Further down the shore
the waves roll in
unrestricted.
The water is translucent
and rainbows are surfing
the crested waves.
The color rolls over the top
of the waves.

Just before the waves reach the shore
the rainbows vanish.

The joy is indescribable.
Does anyone else see this?!
Does this happen all the time
and I never noticed?
Quick! Everyone look!
There is no one close enough to hear.

One particularly perfect wave rolls in
with rainbow riding,
first blue, then green, yellow, and red.
Then all at once the entire wave
and the spray behind it
is awash in violet light.

Tears jump from my eyes,
the heartbreak of something
long forgotten.
Ancient and very important.

As suddenly as the
rainbows appeared
they were gone.
Paddling off to find
another wave.

Trees
by Cyrena Giordano / CYRENITY

Trees
flowing in the breeze
Help me please.
Carry me through

Trees show me please.
Help me see, carry me through

We are strong we are tall.
We are life we are love.
We are here for you whenever you need us.
Just get down on your knees
and give us anything you're
needing to release.

We are here for you

Ooooooooooo

Trees
flowing in the breeze
Help me please.
Carry me through

Trees show me please.
Help me see, carry me through

I am strong I am tall.
I am life I am love.
I know you're here for me
whenever I need you.
I'll get down on my knees
And give you anything
I'm needing to release.
Thank you.

Ooooooooooooo

Trees
flowing in the breeze
Help me please.
Carry me through

Trees show me please.
Help me see, carry me through

I am strong I am tall.
I am life I am love.
I am also here for you
whenever you need me.
I'll get down on my knees
And listen to anything that you
need also, please
I am here for you too.

Oooooooooooo

Trees
flowing in the breeze
Help me please.
Carry me through

Trees show me please.
Help me see, carry me through

A Wildfire has it's Purpose
by Cody Ray Richardson

Are they listening
Are they only filling in the blanks of dialogue in their heads
Do they see me
Do they see their past
Do I fit in to their plan
Are they trying to fit into mine
Do they have a moral compass
Are they just waiting to talk
A pause indicates a lot
Saying nothing sometimes says more
If we knew all the information, would we speak at all
An open hand can be more dangerous then a closed fist
How many times does it take to learn
I trust the sounds of the birds
I cannot understand exactly
Yet, I know what they are saying
Sometimes more than people
I hear their words
Yet, I do not understand
It's easy to feel guilty
After stepping back I realized
They were not talking to me at all
I can't take statements personally that were
merely inner dialogue being expressed
Hearing is easy
Listening is a super power
All the greats know it
Response is always more effective then reaction
Although reaction can mean they care more
It's not inferior to react
In fact it can be more genuine
Does a child respond
We have mostly all been fit into social norms
Some that haven't can come off as being rude
Being unruly
I chose real over thought out
I honor your wild self
Dogs have to be trained to fit in
They are closer to nature
That should tell you something about humans

Nature never fails
Although most of the time we are too selfish to understand
a wildfire and its purpose
I say let it burn
Let it be natural
A tantrum equals a boundary pushed until a person is broken

Let Me Introduce You to my Red-headed Friend
by Karuna McAllister

What if I told you...

Life was around in the form of sound--
Happy is the sound of a Stellar Jay
Squawking and sharing his sky with a Robin.

Cold is not how the salmon feels
as he swims down river like the flow of rain
as it flows down the river and into the sea.

The earth is only as round
as a full moon in the sky.

The Southern Cross and Polaris
are walking down the street holding hands
with a Robin and his Black-headed friend--

They are singing--
"Let me introduce you
to my Red-headed friend!"

A Strong Single Woman
by Christine Jamison

Just because I am a woman
doesn't mean:
that you can walk on me
that you can talk bad to me,
or that I have to listen to you!
I am strong and single.

Just because I am single and a woman
doesn't mean:
that I don't have feelings
that I have to put up with you
that I will not walk away, because
I am strong and single.

Just because I am single, a woman and that I'm strong
doesn't mean:
there aren't any feelings
and
that I will still put you out
because
I can do and be anything, that I want.

OUTER-INNER
by Maria Louisa

Touch IT from the INSIDE
Like colours reflected from the outside:
Inside a crystal globe.

Circulating outer
--with feeling inner.
Absorbed.
Transparent.
ONE.

Hour Glass
by Cody Ray Richardson

It makes no difference
if it's the first or last grain of sand in the hour glass that drops
If unbroken all has its date
No one grain is more significant than the other at the time
Oh how twisted it is to borrow sand from other hour glasses
Breaking the glass in the process
Yet it is the way of this world
This world only being one world
To borrow from other hour glasses is to stay in the way of this world
Letting the sand fall naturally
is to know we are neither the sand nor the hour glass
This is to know the knowing of eternal life

What is, is what will be
by Cody Ray Richardson

Like the light of a star
Your influence felt years later
Still illuminating my mind
So many gaze at a beauty already gone
We all say words of origin unknown
Echos of once was
What now is, from what was
What is, is what will be
Not as aware then as I am now
Now is now
Though then is over now
There really is no over
Only change
Perceived or not

It is what it is
by Cheryl

The foundation of peace is
Acceptance.

Beyond all doors--
there is Expansiveness.

Beyond the division of
borders, gates and locked fences--

there exists the
Innocence of
openness, feeling, kindness

Beyond the
rules, restrictions and requirements
there is
freedom, imagination and spark

Beyond all the opinions and preferences--
there is peace.

There are things that I don't love--
and that is ok.

Accepting All.
It is what it is.

Peace.

Please Keep It
by Cheryl

Please Keep It

What's Left?

Old photos, many
of people I don't
even know.

Smelly quilts and afghans.

Please keep it.

Faded copies of
recipes, unlegible---

Mom's worn and stained
clothes, rusted chains
that were once jewelry.

Please keep it.

I think---
this is my inheritance.

Please keep it.

While others;
friends and family
divide the spoils.

Please keep it.

It's a good thing that someone
loves me.
I have a home and all that I need.

So, Please keep it!

Gone
by Cheryl

Awareness
brings the layers
into focus.
The memories,
a different lifetime.

The mechanic adjusts the dial,
catapulting me
some where---
confusion,
where are the
familiar faces and places
I have grown to love?
Are they gone for good, or will
they return another day?

Here today,
Gone tomorrow

Looking at Flowers
by Zachary Brown

I look into these mirrors to see a reflection,
Instead I get basal base insipid dissection,
Purge the persecution,
Bathe in absolution,
Decay in putrefaction,
Revive the human action,
Becoming a part not apart,
In rhythm imparted by this one beating heart,
We
All
Share
The broke choked joke,
Provoked by bespoke culture,
Creating individual identity, illusory ignominy,
An imitative impatient illness
The barrier to soul
Baring the weight of sins,
Of losses and wins,
Holding on so tight until the heart gives,
And when it does,
burst forth in coronas of love.
Still, afraid to discover itself,
Plant roots,
Shaken,
Grow.
Once no longer afraid to draw outside the lines,
Because straight lines are not wrought naturally
Because in order to be me authentically
I must expose those vulnerable parts of me,
bare roots;
And be the first person to not attack them,
or allow them to harm those in my surroundings;

To see that this,
This me,
This kindness,
This rock,
This tree,
This you,
Is part of me too.

One day, when those roots know they have
already stabilized enough,
Maelstroms will become breezes,
Freezes, a welcome period to rest,
West Summer sun more energy to grow,
Sow the seeds and radiate out in loving
awareness

We are here, together,
on this floating speck,
Infinitesimally small in the scope of it all,

Here's too looking at flowers.

New Cycle of Love
by Cody Ray Richardson

What is voice from divine
What is my mind
What is the residual from what I have eaten
Echos from people
Voices from who knows where
The earth has a frequency
Tune in
Ground
The less I put in
The more the pure frequency is audible
Fast
Cut out the inputs
Lessen the x factors
Calm the waves
Energy is a boomerang
What am I putting out, is
What is coming back
In service I forget my woes
It's not to escape
It's to enter a new cycle
A cycle of love
I'm Sponsored by love
Love has no agenda
No plan
It just gives
Filling in the dents
The rips I've made
The wounds I have allowed
Love is the binder of all things
Lessen the inputs
Let down the shield
Put down the weapons
To allow love in

A Poem to Mount Shasta
by Tara Gardner

Snow silent deep quietude
loud crunching walking in the forest at rest
leaves golden brilliant
showers and frost
summer's intensity
carefree pine needles
golden under my feet

alpine lakes pure bright and cold turning to warm cleansing body
and mind floating on the water held in this mother's, this earth's
womb

winter's green grass and seed sprouting under the snow
bare trees, trees of pine, cedar sap tastes like heaven healing
The last of the blackberries staining my fingers
summer berries, thumb berries, wild strawberries, and raspberries

Wind and trees, owls and silence
hawks and eagles
swarms of migrating orange and black California tortoise shell
butterflies, so many that they block my view when driving up the
mountain
Long hikes with friends, flowers and streams and creeks

The mountain, my dear Mount Shasta, you change
brown mountain, taupe to mauve, snow and golden pink bright in
the sun. Lavender snow and sky

Always at peace, gently powerful
bringing a sudden smile and your peace and
complete joy to all who see you

Dogwoods signal that winter is soon over, first flower white like first
light of the forest I feel childlike joy reminding me to be happy in
my heart to sit on the earth and have my head in the sky and clouds

I love you all
I say to the trees, tell everyone
Light and sparkles twinkling
hovering over the ground
The mountain is. The trees are. The water is. We are. Light.

Bring It!
by Cheryl

Betty Boop
lives like a Queen
in her palace---
a slice of heaven.
Golden drops are her currency;
flitting from flower to flower,
flirting with time,
she says--
"Humans, you need to raise the bar.
Bring your Best Bee game!"

Bee Kind.
Bee Honest.
Bee Free.

Inspiration for this poem came from Mt. Shasta's local beekeeper, Mariana Riquelme Harmon and a dream message she received.

Earth Day Gratitude
by Patricia Carreras

Such Gratitude to Moma Earth
for her love, caring compassion
and nurturing abundance.

Our existence would not be possible
without her refreshing waters;
her fruits, trees and flowers of the field;
and
her breath of air, clouds and rains.

Thank you Moma

Hawkwomyn ~
by Mercy Talley

I identify :
as a bird
that's why
I soar above
the herd

Hawkwomyn ~

the Sky
Is Free so
Come
Join me

where

the Vista
Enthralls
& dilemmas
become small

here

Our Spirits
Take Wing so
Our Souls'
Can Sing

and

sagas
resolve
with
Sunset's
Splendor ~

Owl by Dave Harvey

Silent wings unfurl,
Secrets held in moonlit eyes,
Wisdom takes to flight.

Not Without Choosing
by Connie Bonner-Britt
Turtle Woman
Spo- pi- Aakii

Blackfeet name,
gifted by sister,
Cheryl Ibarra
Piegan Woman
Pikuni Aakii

Let's not Forget.
Each day is a Ceremony.
Each day is Holy.
Healing continues through Awareness.
The Earth Day Celebrations are not over.
Planting seeds is Eternal.
Our ancestral Grandmothers sewed them into the hems of their skirts.
Over seas, through famine, and land migration...often forced against their will.
Yet they knew.
Healing is an Act of Resistance.
Not without choosing.
Taught from one generation to the next.
Prayers for Peace and Reconciliation must carry forward with each heart,
into each new day.
Through all our actions toward each other.
In all we choose to be.
Astrology says we are in a New Day.
New Energy, Higher Consciousness is showering.
Strong upon us.
Ancient Indigenous Prophecy...is Now they say.
Full Pink Moon today.
Pluto aligned with Uranus.
Reflection, Meditation, Realignment.
Each day is a Ceremony of Healing.
Not without choosing.

Replenishing
by Jennifer Hershelman

Sitting silent in the woods
a gentle breeze brushes by your face
its not the wind
the trees are breathing all around you

Breathing life into the world,
      Replenishing

Standing, silently, crying against a trunk
-sweet release, ease the energy out

Trees

Soaking in your tears, your fears
Holding space for all your pain
with nothing to gain

But a song, of love and gratitude
      Replenishing
Necessary.

For the space they hold
for us all

Standing tall
beacons of energy

Anchoring in reality

Shifting the winds

Swirling the world
into
Peace and balance.

Experience
by Cody Ray Richardson

The experience that nearly killed you
Saved you too
Because you made the change it suggested
You changed the rules
Some things just can't be forgiven by some
Moving on is their only option
Some battles can't be won
Other times people change us
They may give us another chance
We may choose not to take it
We may give up
What does that say about the moments
In them can we keep trust
From experience to experience
Our wisdom grows
Still, can we stay in discernment
At the doorway of perceptions, hold
Put down our weapons
Open up our hearts
Or allow the past to rip now apart
Will be is determined by frequency
As big as it is
Captains navigate the sea
The internal abyss is easy to drown in

Nature serves to keep us here
When I enter her playground
All troubles disappear
Here in my treehouse I found my ease
Holding her tightly
With my feet in her water
I snuggle her trees

Many thanks to these contributors:

Wolf Martinez

A'Marie B. Thomas-Brown

Cody Ray Richardson

Maria Louisa

Mary Schrack

David Kolden

Barbara Bader

Julie Bailey

Mercy Talley

Tara Gardner

Cyrena Giordana/CYRENITY

Karuna McAllister

Christine Jamison

Zachary Brown

Connie Bonner-Britt Blackfeet name gifted by sister,
Turtle Woman Cheryl Ibarra
Spo- pi- Aakii Piegan Woman
  Pikuni Aakii

Jennifer Hershelman

Patricia Carreras

Dave Harvey

Will Gaines

Richard Jefferies

Author page--

Cheryl Lunar Wind lives in the Mount Shasta area in a little town called Weed. She is a practicer of Mayan cosmology, Lakota ceremony, Star Knowledge and the Universal Laws including the Law of One. Her hobbies are writing poetry, music, dance, drum circles and love for all life; plant, animal and crystal. Cheryl has been a guide and spiritual teacher for many years. Now she shares wit and wisdom through poetry, and has published poetry books; Know Your Way, We Are One, Follow the White Rabbit, Love Your Light, LIFE: Shared thru Poetry, Come to Mount Shasta: Sacred Path Poetry, We Are Light, Finding Our Way Home, We Are Forever, Handshake With the Divine, Grand Rising: A New Day Has Dawned, Star Messages: Codes to Sing, Dance and Live by, Return to Innocence, and Bloom Like Nature: Live the Natural Way.

Testimonials---

"Cheryl's poetry is very inspiring--particularly the way she compares life with the forces of nature. There is a special element in her poems that opens my heart and fills my soul with divine possiblities."
Giovanna Taormina, Co-Founder, One Circle Foundation

"Cheryl's poems have helped me to uncover and honor my own hidden memories. The beauty of her spirit is evident in each tender, insightful passage."
Marguerite Lorimer, www.earthalive.com

"A rare collection filled with raw, courageous honesty. Thought provoking words that
will stop you in your tracks."
Snow Thorner, ED Open Sky Gallery, Montague, California

"When wisdom, guidance, confirming comfort, ect. arrives to us humans--from beings with the perspective of other realms--it is a divine gift. Especially in the form of what we call poetry, and through a being with no agenda; Cheryl Lunar Wind simply shares what source gives her!"--Dragon Love (Thomas) Budde

Cheryl,
Greetings and Happy Monday to you my friend. I just wanted to share with you that every time I read 'Come to Mount Shasta', even now that I'm mentioning it I cry, I cannot help it, it is such a Divine message and so impeccable in its timing. I came up here for Spirit, you know I was called by Source and I live on the mountain and I just want to thank you. Your poem found me last summer at the headwaters during the Alien and Angels conference; and then I found your book sitting in the gazebo and I just can't stop, I love it! I love you, thank you.
---Jim

Cheryl,
Just want to thank you for your bringing me into the community at Shasta. What you are doing/did do is absolutely changing my life. You did it, you were instrumental in helping me set my true path. Spirit is moving and the more of us that listen and act the sooner the shift will be completed.
---Darrel

About Cheryl's poetry--
"You are dynamic! I have known no one who does so much so swiftly, and your writing touches my heart because it comes from your heart."
---The Durwood Show

"Your words are my words. I keep your book 'Know Your Way' on my nightstand. I read it at bedtime and morning."
---Karina Arroyo

"Cheryl's words work magic in my heart, stirring the wisdom that is buried so deeply within me---beautiful indeed!"
---Ellie Pfeiffer, founder of Ellie's Espresso & Bakery, Weed, CA

www.ingramcontent.com/pod-product-compliance
Lightning Source LLC
Chambersburg PA
CBHW061255040426

42444CB00010B/2386